SCHIRMER'S LIBRARY
OF MUSICAL CLASSICS

Vol. 489

F. MAZAS

Seventy-Five Melodious and Progressive Studies

Op. 36

For Violin

IN THREE BOOKS

ISBN 978-0-7935-3683-2

G. SCHIRMER, Inc.

DISTRIBUTED BY

HAL•LEONARD®
CORPORATION

7777 W. BLUEMOUND RD. P.O. BOX 13819 MILWAUKEE, WI 53213

Artists' Studies

F. MAZAS Op. 36, Book 3

4

The chords with down-bow, generally from the nut.

60.

10

Allegro leggiero.

61.

Introduction.
Andante.

In this exercise all chords are to be taken with **down-bow,** and from the nut.

Allegro marziale.

Coda.
Allegro.

Più vivace.

Allegro moderato.

Tempo I. (*Allegro moderato.*)

Andante con moto.

64.

Allegro.

Tarentella.
Allegro vivace.

65.

Tremolo with bow on string. *(not springing.)*

67.

Exercise on the Tremolo legato.

(Rapidly repeated finger-stroke in *legato* playing.)

The half-note indicates the finger which executes the trill. Practise slowly at first, and observe throughout the value of the notes as written out in the first four measures of the *Andante*.

Tremolo with springing bow.

Introduction.
Poco Adagio.

69.

Arpeggio exercise.

On three strings.

Practise, at first, with simple detached bowing, middle of bow, very short, and without quitting the string, and marking the bass notes. In the second style, the springing bow sounds two tones both with down-bow and with up-bow.

The preceding exercise, with three notes instead of two.

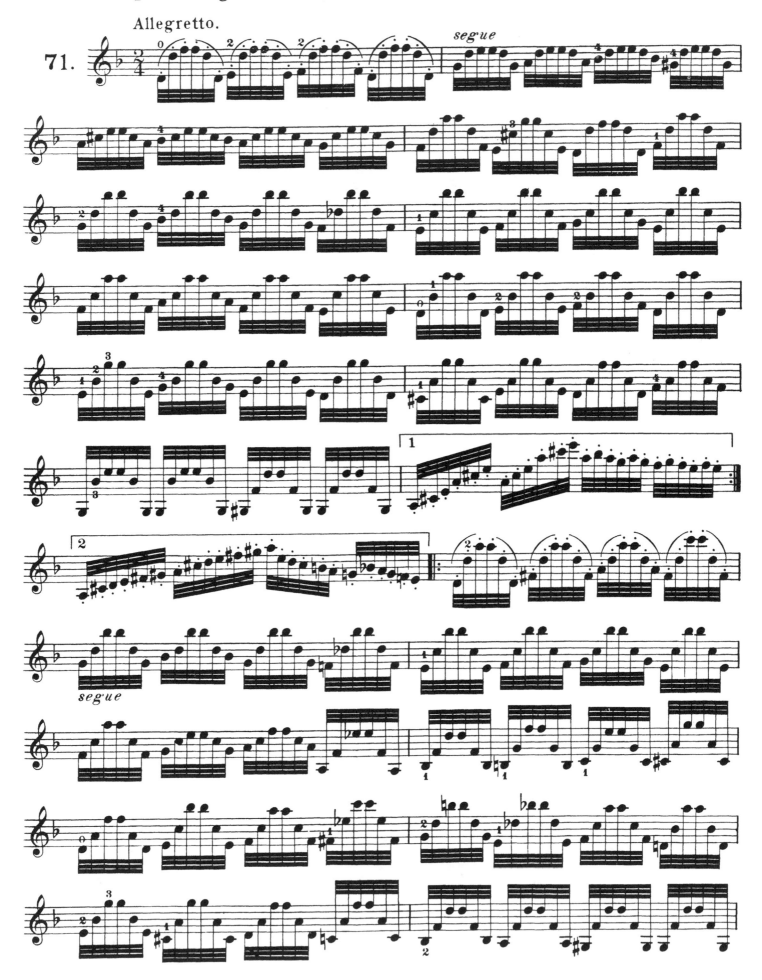

Legato Arpeggios.

Arpeggios of three notes, on the four strings.

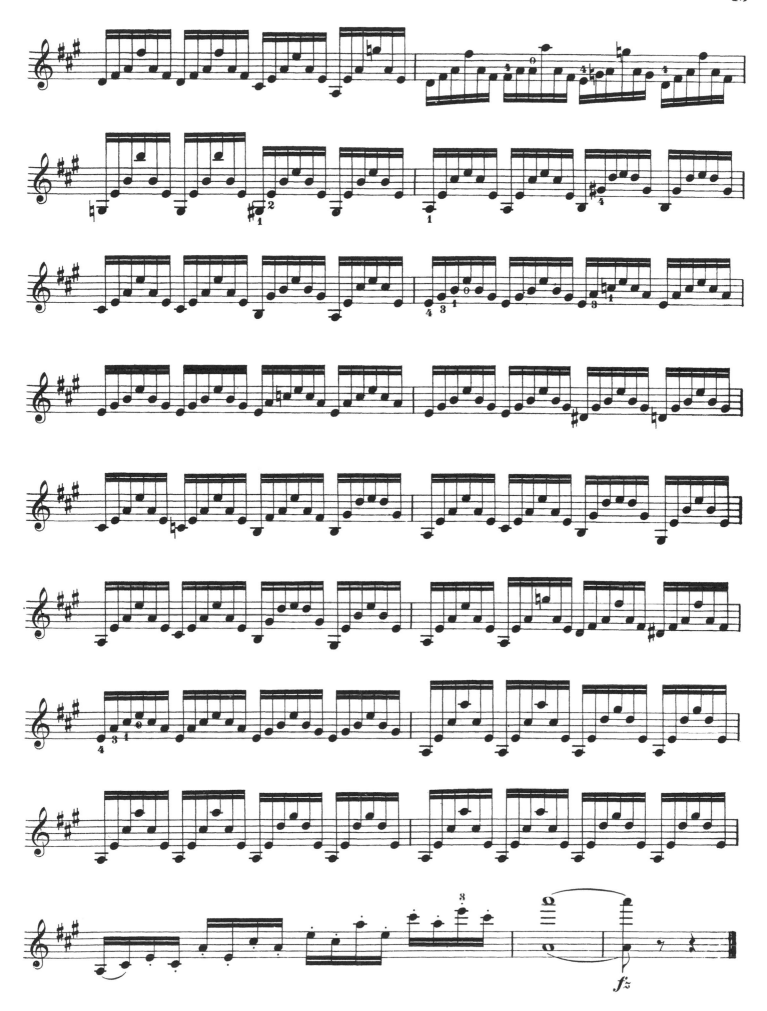

Arpeggios of four notes on the four strings.

Play this study with a firm bow, without quitting the string, and accent each first note in the groups of four.

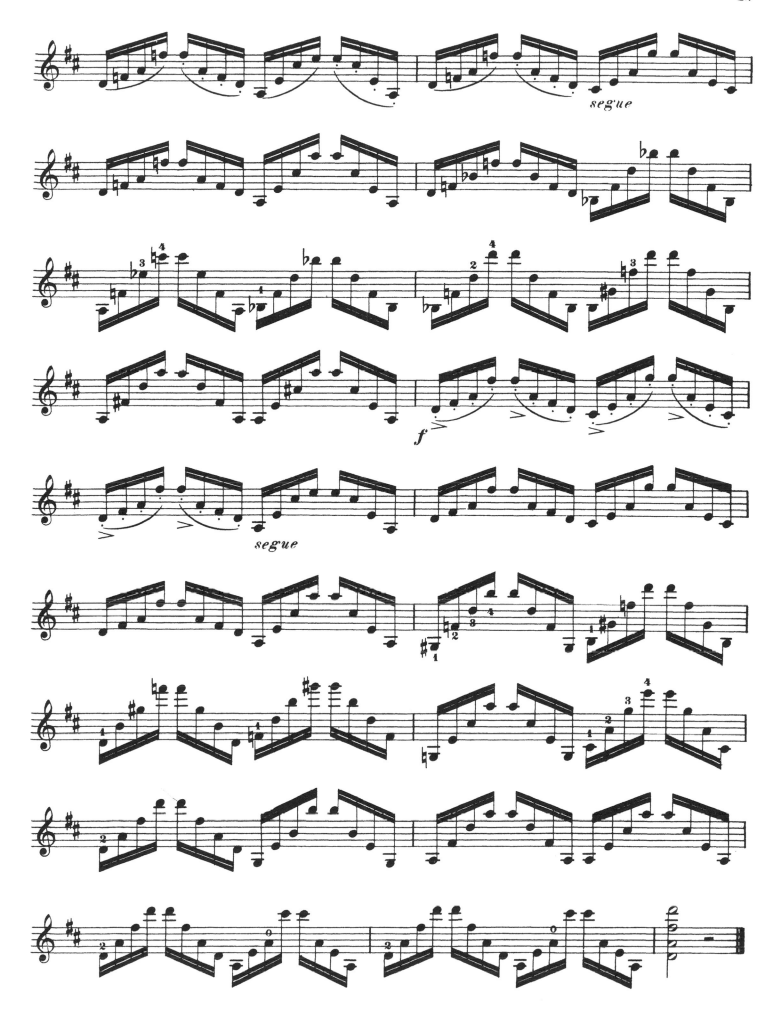

Maestoso sostenuto.

75.

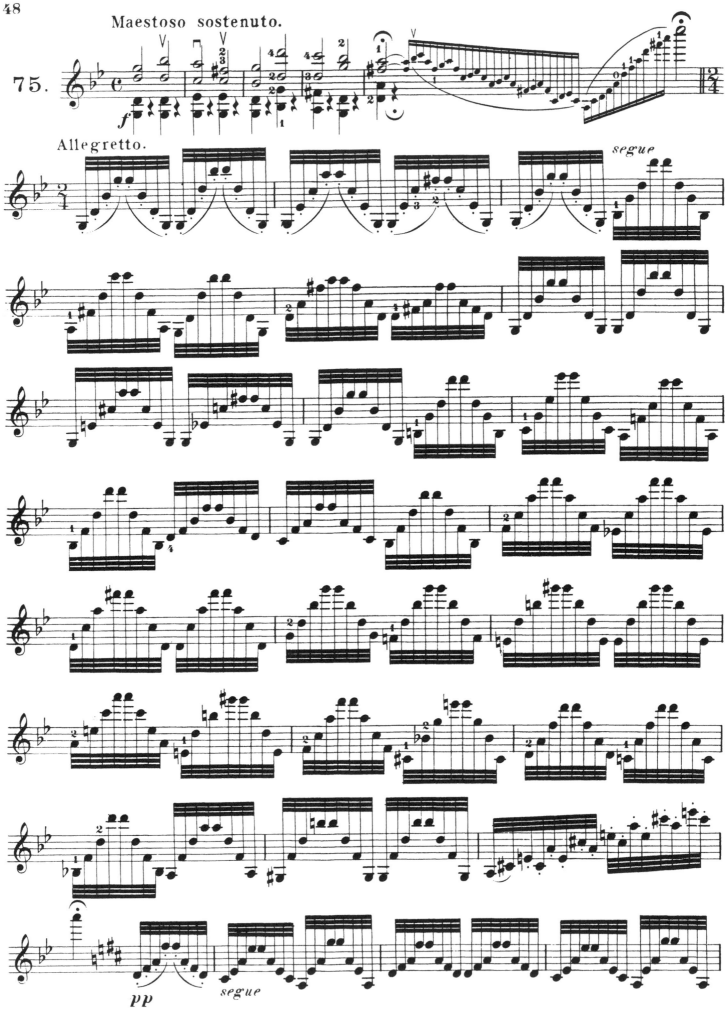

Allegretto.

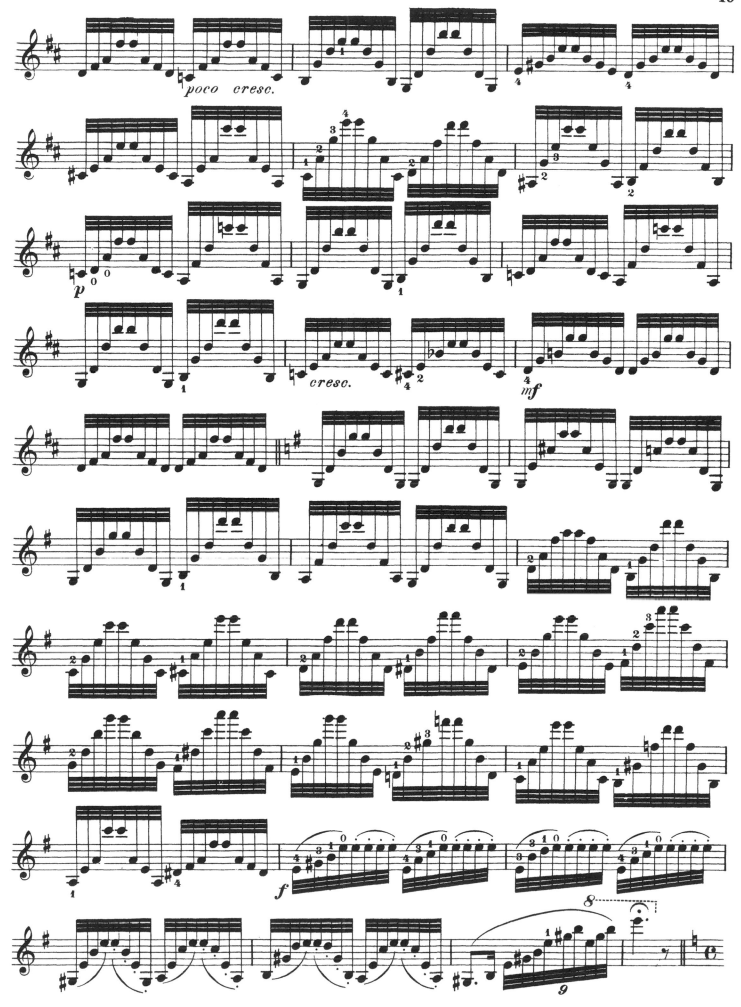